Bible Places

A handbook for the visitor to the Holy Land

John Walden

A Division of GL Publications
Ventura, CA U.S.A.

Co-edition arranged with the help of Angus Hudson, London.

THE PURPOSE OF THIS BOOK

The pilgrim's short stay in the Holy Land will be memorable. Each stone he sees, each view that is carried back home in the camera, each place visited, is crammed with biblical history.

As the experienced guide unwinds the history, and as your pilgrimage leader expounds the scriptural significance, so you will want to be able to turn quickly to the relevant Bible passage. This is the sole purpose of this book. It is essentially a handy pilgrimage Bible handbook to the places visited by most Holy Land tours.

This explains why some things do not get mentioned and others are treated 'thinly'. There is no time to read pages of information about each site, while you are on location. Later, because of your visit to the places where God unfolded the drama of salvation, you will, it is hoped, be stimulated to delve into deeper study. On page 90 there is a list of books that will be of help.

I wish to record my gratitude to Cyril Hadler for encouraging me to compile this book, and to Mrs Sainsbury for being a patient copy typist.

Thousands of pilgrims have used this handbook in a previous edition, and this new colour edition contains updated additional information, following helpful comments from users.

Eph 3:16–21 *John Walden*

Original edition first published 1975
New colour edition first published 1984

ISBN 0 86065-233-5

Printed in Great Britain for
KINGSWAY PUBLICATIONS LTD
Lottbridge Drove, Eastbourne, E. Sussex BN23 6NT by
Purnell & Sons Ltd

North American Edition Including Canada
Published by Regal Books
A Division of G/L Publications
Ventura, California, USA

LIST OF ABBREVIATIONS

The names of Bible books have been abbreviated according to the list below.

The Old Testament

Gen	*Genesis*
Ex	*Exodus*
Lev	*Leviticus*
Num	*Numbers*
Deut	*Deuteronomy*
Josh	*Joshua*
Judg	*Judges*
Ruth	*Ruth*
1 Sam	*1 Samuel*
2 Sam	*2 Samuel*
1 Kings	*1 Kings*
2 Kings	*2 Kings*
1 Chron	*1 Chronicles*
2 Chron	*2 Chronicles*
Ezra	*Ezra*
Neh	*Nehemiah*
Esther	*Esther*
Job	*Job*
Ps	*Psalms*
Prov	*Proverbs*
Eccles	*Ecclesiastes*
Song	*Song of Solomon*
Is	*Isaiah*
Jer	*Jeremiah*
Lam	*Lamentations*
Ezek	*Ezekiel*
Dan	*Daniel*
Hos	*Hosea*
Joel	*Joel*
Amos	*Amos*
Obad	*Obadiah*
Jon	*Jonah*
Mic	*Micah*
Nahum	*Nahum*
Hab	*Habakkuk*
Zeph	*Zephaniah*
Hag	*Haggai*
Zech	*Zechariah*
Mal	*Malachi*

The New Testament

Mt	*Matthew*
Mk	*Mark*
Lk	*Luke*
Jn	*John*
Acts	*Acts*
Rom	*Romans*
1 Cor	*1 Corinthians*
2 Cor	*2 Corinthians*
Gal	*Galatians*
Eph	*Ephesians*
Phil	*Philippians*
Col	*Colossians*
1 Thess	*1 Thessalonians*
2 Thess	*2 Thessalonians*
1 Tim	*1 Timothy*
2 Tim	*2 Timothy*
Tit	*Titus*
Philem	*Philemon*
Heb	*Hebrews*
Jas	*James*
1 Pet	*1 Peter*
2 Pet	*2 Peter*
1 Jn	*1 John*
2 Jn	*2 John*
3 Jn	*3 John*
Jude	*Jude*
Rev	*Revelation*

DATELINE

Some words are used in this book that may not be familiar to the Christian who struggles to get dates and places in their historical and geographical perspective. Words like *exile* and *pre-conquest*, and some places that have had several different names, can make it all a bit confusing. To help, here is a short history of Bible events.

Time	What happened	What survives	What the Bible teaches
Before 2000 B.C.	Events as told in *Gen 1–11.*		That God is the author and the sustainer of life.
About 2000–1200 B.C.	Abraham, Isaac, Jacob, Joseph, Moses.	The Cave in Hebron, believed to be the tombs of the patriarchs.	God provides, *Gen 22:14*
	The patriarchs settle in the land and then migrate to Egypt, the exodus and wilderness wanderings.	Jacob's well in Samaria.	God guards his people, *Deut 7:6f.* God requires a response, *Ex 20:3.*
About 1200–1050 B.C.	Return to the Promised Land and tribes begin to settle into autonomous units.	The Hebrew language. Ten Commandments. Some town and village names.	Struggle to continue believing *Josh 1:13, Judg 2:10.*

Time	What happened	What survives	What the Bible teaches
About 1050–930 B.C.	The people wanted a king like other nations. Saul chosen. David is the great king uniting the country. Solomon builds first temple. The nation splits into two–Judah in south and Israel in north.	Early books of Bible. Many archaeological sites in Jerusalem, Samaria and Megiddo.	Prophets begin to tell of God's judgement if idolatry (worship of another god) continues, *1 Sam 8:7*. Social justice begins to be stressed.
930–538 B.C.	Israel and Judah war with each other. Assyrians capture north and take people off into captivity 722 B.C. Babylonians take Judah into captivity 587 B.C. Some Jews return in 538 B.C.	Books of later prophets. Samaritans and their beliefs. The synagogue system of teaching.	There is the perennial complaint, *Hos 4:1*. God is continually gracious to his people. A relationship with him does not depend on heredity alone, *Ezek 18:21*. New behaviour will develop, *Ezek 36:22f*.
538 B.C. –19 B.C.	2nd temple began to be built in Jerusalem. Ezra/Nehemiah supervise. The Greek rulers of Egypt (Ptolemies) conquer the land. Maccabean revolt. Herod begins 3rd temple 19 B.C.	Old Testament completed. Dead Sea scrolls written by Armenian community. The Western wall in Jerusalem. Masada. Great number of archaeological remains.	A consistent life is best. *Neh 9:33,38*.

Time	What happened	What survives	What the Bible teaches
19 B.C. – A.D. 70	Life of Christ. B.C. 6 (?) to A.D. 27. Christian expansion. Jewish revolt against Rome. Jerusalem sacked, and temple destroyed A.D. 70.	Walls around Jerusalem.	Jesus came for a purpose, *Mt 1:21*. He sees the end of a 'kingdom on earth' dream, *Mt 24:1–2*.
66-70 395-637 637	Jewish revolt against Roman occupation. Byzantine occupation Arab conquest.	Basilica in Bethlehem. Dome of the Rock. Hisham's Palace, Jericho.	
1099-1291 1291-1516 1516-1917 1870 1909 1917 1948 1956 1967 1973	Crusaders from Europe. Mameluk period. Turkish Ottoman empire annexes Holy Land. Jewish pioneers begin resettlement. Tel Aviv founded. British mandate begins. State of Israel established. Sinai Campaign. Six Day War. Day of Atonement War.		

The Roman emperors of the New Testament era

31 B.C. – 14 A.D.	Augustus Caesar
A.D. 13-37	Tiberius Caesar
A.D. 37-41	Caligula
A.D. 41-54	Claudius
A.D. 54-68	Nero
A.D. 68-69	Galba
A.D. 69	Otho and Vitellius
A.D. 69-79	Vespasian
A.D. 79-81	Titus
A.D. 81-96	Domitian

Name

The biblical name is *Kiriath Jearim* which means 'a city of the forests'. Abu Ghosh was a brigand of the 19th century.

Bible references

It was once one of the chief cities of the tribe of Gibeon *Josh 9:17*. It also marked the border between the territory of Judah and Benjamin *Josh 15:60*. Called Kiriath-baal in *Josh 15:60*, this could mean that Canaanite idolatrous worship had taken place there. Other names are Baale-judah *2 Sam 6:2* and Kiriath-arim *Ezra 2:25*.

The ark arrived here after its return from the Philistines *1 Sam 7:1*. King David collected the ark and took it in triumph into Jerusalem *2 Sam 6:2, 1 Chron 13:5*. Uriah, a prophet in the time of Jeremiah, also lived here *Jer 26:20*. Kiriath had its repatriates from the exile *Neh 7:29*. Could also be site of Emmaus.

History

The village has had a long history of being a 'border town'. It witnessed the first victory during the 1967 Israeli War of Independence. In Roman times a detachment from the 10th Legion built a military post to guard the road from Jerusalem.

What to see

An old Jewish cemetery. The ruins of the ancient 'Castellum Romanum'.

ACRE

Acre. old Crusader fortifications

Name

The biblical name is *Akko.*

Bible references

Judg 1:31 gives the area to the tribe of Asher. The tribe failed to capture it. The seaport probably remained in Phoenician hands throughout the Old Testament period.

Acts 21:7. Towards the end of Paul's third missionary journey, his coastal ship called in to Ptolemais, its name at that time, whilst in transit from Tyre to Caesarea.

History

Ancient walled town with natural position for a harbour, defended by Phoenicians for centuries. The town has withstood 17 sieges including those of Simon Maccabaeus and Napoleon. Richard the Lionheart captured the town during his crusade.

What to see

El Jazzar's Wall, Municipal Museum, Crypt of St John of Knights Hospitallers (second oldest example of Gothic architecture in the world).

Acre. fishermen's harbour

ANATHOTH

Location
Small village on the road from Jerusalem to Nablus, approx. 2 miles from city boundary.
Bible reference
Jeremiah the prophet lived here *Jer 29:27.*

ARAD

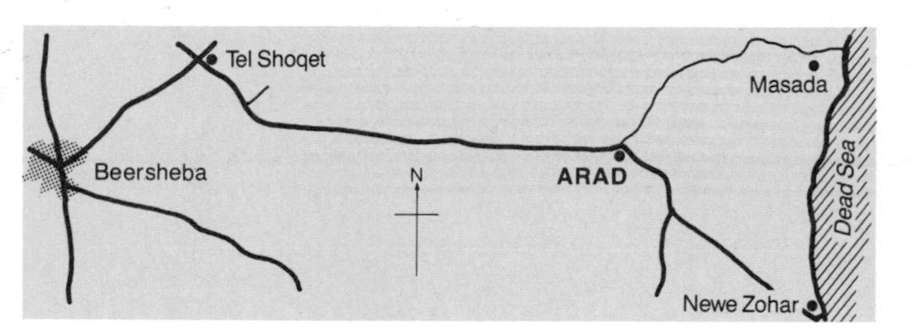

Location
On the Dead Sea road to Beersheba in the Negev.
Bible references
Num 21:1-3 describes an Israelite victory, as does *Josh 12:14.* Shishak, a famous Egyptian king, conquered all this territory after the death of Solomon *2 Chron 12:2f.*
History
A climb of 3300 feet from the Dead Sea, through shimmering desert, brings us to a city amidst a desert. Here green grass grows and there are swimming pools.

Reconstruction began in 1961, and this is already a rejuvenated city.

What to see

Travelling along the Dead Sea to Beersheba, the tourist can stop for lunch in an air-conditioned hotel.

ASHDOD

Name

Azotis in Greek, Isdud in Arabic.

Location

A main port south of Tel Aviv.

Bible references

Judah failed to conquer it *Josh 13:3.* The Philistines had a temple to the god Dagon (Neptune) there *1 Sam 5:1.* Amos prophesied about it *Amos 1:8.*

Partially repatriated after the exile *Neh 13:23*. Azotus, *Acts 8:40*, is identified as the place to which Philip returned after baptizing the eunuch.

History

Main Philistine port, but conquered by each succeeding onslaught in subsequent history.

The town was on the great inter-continental road trade route between Asia and Africa.

ASHKELON

Ashkelon, Old City Wall

Location
On the coast between Gaza and Ashdod.

Bible references
David lamented over the death of Saul *2 Sam 1:20*, because Saul had committed suicide after a Philistine defeat.

Zeph 2:4 tells of the prophet's woe for that area. A prophecy of the future was spoken *Zeph 2:7*.

History
Known as a centre for rebellion as long ago as the 14th century B.C., according to the Tel-el-Amarna letters. The Egyptians captured the city and later the Philistines used it as their main port. The Philistines raided inland into Israelite territory from here.

Each wave of invaders conquered it. Our word 'shallot', for a special type of onion, originates from the Roman word 'ascalonia'. This vegetable made the district famous in ancient times!

shkelon. National Park excavations

What to see
The National Park is famous for its picnic area. Beautiful beach. Ruins of a 6th-century Byzantine church.

AYALON

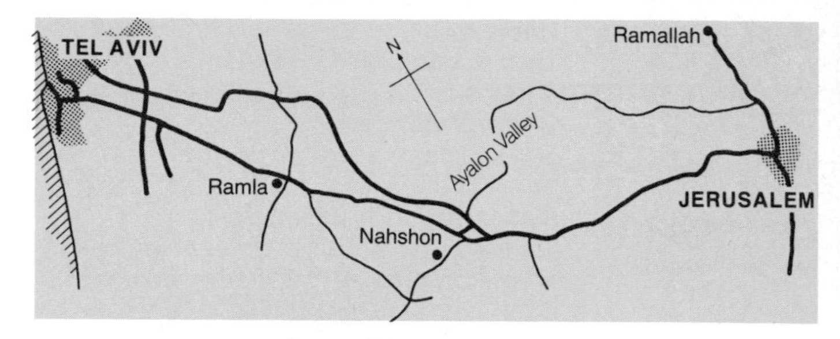

Location
A valley on the left after leaving Ramla on the Tel Aviv–Jerusalem road.
Bible reference
Josh 10:12 tells of Joshua praying to God for extra time to defeat an enemy.
History
Judas Maccabaeus gathered troops here, as did the Roman legions on their way to destroy Jerusalem. The Crusaders used the valley as a resting place on the way to conquer the city for Christianity.

BEATITUDES, MOUNT OF

Location
On a hill on north-western shore of Galilee, in the foothills, near Capernaum.
Bible reference
Traditionally the site where Jesus preached his famous sermon of which the most memorable sayings are recorded *Mt 5–7*.

What to see
On the slope of the hill is a black domed octagonal church. There is a magnificent view overlooking the lake.

Mount of Beatitudes and Sea of Galilee

BEERSHEBA

Name
Means 'well of the oath' *Gen 21:31*.

Location
A town in the Negev desert at an important crossroads, on the road to Eilat, 48 miles south-west of Jerusalem.

Bible references
The main reason why there has been settlement here is its well *Gen 21:14*, *Josh 19:2*. Although 4000 years old, the well still exists. Beersheba has a population of 85,000 today. Abraham spent some time here *Gen 22:19*. It was from here that he set out in obedience to God, to be prepared to sacrifice Isaac. The land was apportioned to the tribe of Simeon *Josh 19:2*.

What to see
In the Old Town, there is Abraham's Well and the Bedouin Market on Thursdays from 6–9 a.m.

Beersheba. Bedouin market

BEITSHEAM

Name
Means 'house of gates'.
Location
11 miles from Haifa on the Afula road.
What to see
There is a most important Jewish archaeological site of the ancient city. In the 2nd century the Sanhedrin (Supreme Court) had its seat here. Rabbi Hanassi, the compiler of the Mishna literature, lived here.

The Catacombs There are about 200 sarcophagi here with interesting carvings.

The Olive Press This site is well worth a visit to gain valuable background information on Jewish life in post-Bible times.

Ruins of Synagogue Built in the 2nd century and destroyed by the Romans in 352. It was perhaps the largest synagogue in the country.

BETHANY

Bethany, tomb of Lazarus

Name
Elzariya (Arabic for Lazarus).
Location
On the Jerusalem–Jericho road, just outside the city boundary. On the east slope of the Mount of Olives *Jn 11:18*. The ancient village was probably a little higher up the hill than the present one.
Bible references
The friends of Jesus, Mary, Martha and Lazarus lived here *Jn 11:5, 12:1*.

Bethany, tomb of Lazarus

Lazarus was raised from the dead. Jesus reminds Martha not to be anxious *Lk 10.40*. Jesus was anointed *Mk 14:3f*.

What to see

A new Roman Catholic church with a beautiful mosaic depicting the raising of Lazarus. In the grounds are remains of Roman, Byzantine and Crusader times. Ask attendant to visit the wine press. A 'tomb of Lazarus' is nearby.

BETHLEHEM

Name

Means 'house of bread'. Also ancient Ephrathah *Gen. 35:19* and Bethlehem Judah to distinguish it from Bethlehem in the northern part of the tribal conquests *Josh 19:15*.

Location

6 miles from Jerusalem, just off the main road to Hebron.

Bible references

Jacob buried Rachel here *Gen. 48:7*. The love story of Ruth and Boaz happened in adjacent fields *Ruth 1.22*. David had his home here *1 Sam 16:4, 13*. Whilst away fighting, David asked for water from his home well *1 Chron 11:16f*.

Prophecy of the birth of the Messiah *Mic 5:2*. Jesus was born in Bethlehem *Mt 2:1*. Herod had the town's little children executed *Mt 2:16*.

Bethlehem, market scene

History

A quiet country town whose claim for attention is around the two kings–David

Bethlehem, Ruth and Boaz fields

and Jesus. Christians revered a cave as the birthplace of Jesus after the 2nd century. During the Persian conquest in the 7th century, they spared the ancient church because they found a mosaic depicting the Magi in Persian dress.

What to see

The Church of Nativity
In Manger Square, it is claimed to be the oldest existing Christian church in the world. Constructed in A.D. 325.

Much additional building has been taking place over 16 centuries. Jerome translated the Bible into Latin here about A.D. 380. The 'Door of Humility' prevented people riding into the church on horseback. Roman Catholic, Greek Orthodox and Armenian Christians share the church.

David's Wells
These are on the right as you enter Bethlehem from Jerusalem. Opposite is a splendid view overlooking the Shepherds' fields and the Herodium. David longed to drink water, whilst on the run. *2 Sam 23:15.*

Helen Keller Home
With other orphanages, a centre of Christian work.

BETHPHAGE

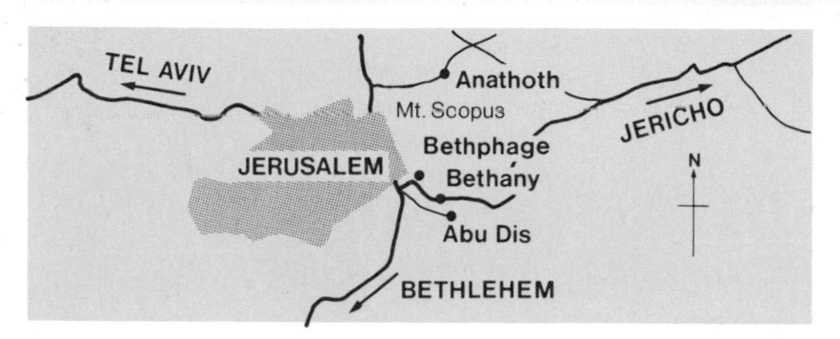

Name

Abu Dis.

Location

A village on the Mount of Olives, near the Jerusalem–Jericho road, very close to Bethany.

Bible references

Mt 21:1, Lk 19:29. In Bible times, the village was technically within the boundary of Jerusalem and so pilgrims at the Passover Festival could virtually claim to reside in the Holy City. It is thought that Jesus began his triumphant entry into Jerusalem from here *Mk 11:1.*

What to see

Enjoy a walk from the top of the Mount of Olives down to Bethany, and trace the route taken by Jesus down the only footpath.

The Greek Orthodox church built on the site of the Crusader church.

Bethlehem, Church of the Nativity bells

BETHSAIDA

Location
A place on the northern shore of Galilee, near Capernaum.

Bible reference
After the feeding of the 5000, Jesus set out in a boat for the town *Mk 6:45*.

CAESAREA

Caesarea, aqueduct

Location
On the coastal road midway between Haifa and Tel Aviv.

Bible references
This was the home of Philip the Evangelist *Acts 21:8*. Cornelius the centurion lived here also *Acts 10:1,24, Acts 11:11*. Here Peter had understanding of his vision about the entry of Gentiles into the kingdom of God *Acts 10:35*. Paul was sent for trial from here *Acts 23:23*.

History
Another city built by Herod the Great, this time built right on the Mediterranean shore. He named it after the Emperor Caesar Augustus. The Romans used it as their main base, building magnificent stone breakwaters for the harbour.

Being a city with a mixed population, there were clashes of a racial nature. During the Jewish uprising of A.D. 66, 20,000 Jews were massacred. It was the start of the destruction of the Jewish state, finished in

A.D. 70 by the destruction of the temple in Jerusalem.

What to see

The remains of the aqueduct, the archaeological remains of the city including the magnificent statues, the reconstructed amphitheatre, the stone bearing the inscription 'Pontius Pilate'. This inscription gives further proof of Pilate's existence, apart from references to him in the Gospels and the writings of historians such as Josephus.

Caesarea, reconstructed amphitheatre

CAESAREA PHILIPPI

Location

A place at the foot of Mount Hermon north of Galilee, adjacent to the source of the river Jordan. The village is now called Banias, in the district of the Golan Heights.

Bible reference

Probably the place of Peter's confession *Mt 16:13f.*

CANA

Cana, street scene

Name

Cana could derive from the Hebrew *kanah* which means 'a reed', hence 'Cana in Galilee'.

Location

There are two possible sites, Kafr Kana is only 6 miles from Nazareth and on the Haifa-Tiberias road. It is more easily accessible, and has stronger claims than Chisbet Kana, which is 9 miles from Nazareth.

Bible references

The first miracle of Jesus happened here *Jn 2:1f.* An official from Capernaum sought Jesus here and asked his help *Jn 4:46f.* Also the home of Nathaniel *Jn 21:2.*

What to see

A Roman Catholic church with two towers and a red dome, built to commemorate the miracle.

Cana, type of water pot (see Jn 2)

CAPERNAUM

Name

The Hebrew name is *Kefar Nahum,* which means 'village of Nahum'. Tell Hum is Arabic.

Location

On the north shore of Lake Galilee.

Bible references

After leaving Nazareth where he grew up, Jesus settled here *Mk 2:1, Mt 9:1.* This fulfilled a prophecy *Mt 4:13.* Jesus was in the habit of attending the synagogue *Mk 1:21*. Jesus healed Peter's mother-in-law here *Mk 1:30* and healed others at the close of a busy day *Mk 1:32*. In thanksgiving, a centurion built a synagogue *Lk 7:5*. Strong words from Jesus about the city came true *Mt 11:23*.

History

Capernaum was an important border town with a customs post. It stood on the main trade route from Damascus to the coast and on to Egypt. Jesus made the town the centre of his Galilean ministry. The site was hidden until excavations in 1920 uncovered some magnificent ruins. All this makes the place very important to Christian pilgrims.

What to see

An octagonal shaped building
This may be a ruin of an ancient church. It is labelled as 'St Peter's House'.

Carvings
Carvings of the olive tree, symbol of Israel. The designs on Israel's coins came from these. Also a carving of the ark of covenant. Look for the five-pointed Star of David carving.

Capernaum, symbol carvings

The Synagogue

Capernaum, ancient Jewish synagogue

A most important archaeological find. There are three things to notice. The *stone* is different from the local 'black' volcanic rock and must have been transported here. It is of advanced *design* for a 2nd-century synagogue because of the flight of stairs. It is thought that this building would have been erected on the site of the one of Christ's day. Look hard for the *money changers' bowls* at the entrance steps. Being a border town meant brisk business.

CARMEL

Name

Karm-El means 'the vineyards of him' or 'fruitful land'.

Location

A range of hills whose maximum height is 1740 feet, stretching from Haifa 30 miles inland, curving south. Traffic is forced to go through at only four passes.

Mt Carmel from Megiddo

Bible references

The ridge acted as a border between tribes *Josh 19:26*. Elijah's famous contest between his God and Baal happened either near the present village of El-Muhraka or near Isfaya *1 Kings 18:21f*. Amos the country prophet preached here *Amos 9:3*. Isaiah knew of the luxuriant growth on its slopes *Is 35:2*. Jeremiah uses Carmel as a contrast between foes *Jer 46:18*.

History

Because of the many caverns, this ridge has been occupied since the Stone Age. Carmel is mentioned in Egyptian writings. Haifa is the main focal point and blossomed quickly under Jewish immigration.

What to see

Within the city boundaries of Haifa are:

The Druze village of Isfiya 8 miles on the road to Meggido. The Druze are very colourful people.

Bahai Temple This is the centre of this Persian Bahai sect founded in 1850 by Mirza Ali Mohammed.

Elijah's Cave He is supposed to have taken refuge here.

DEAD SEA

Location

In the south-east of Israel, at the south end of the river Jordan. It is the border between Israel and Jordan.

Bible references

Several names are used – Salt Sea *Gen 14:3;* the Eastern Sea *Ezek 47:18;* Sea of Arabah *Deut 3:17.*

The Dead Sea, salt crystals

Sodom and Gomorrah had a terrible fate *Gen 19:24f* and Lot's wife suffered too *Gen 19:26*.

The Dead Sea acted as a border between tribes *Josh 15:2,5*. A prophet used the Sea as an example of judgement *Zeph 2:9*. Ezekiel saw a vision of the sea being made into a 'living sea' *Ezek 47:7,12*.

Features

The level of water is 1291 feet below sea level. The deepest point is 1300 feet below this figure. The size is approx. 48 × 12 miles. Evaporation is so intense that despite being fed from four sources the water level remains constant.

The water has eight times the concentration of salt of ordinary sea water. Other chemicals found in the water are potash, magnesium, calcium, chloride and bromide. The Israeli government are developing thriving chemical industries.

The content of the water explains the buoyancy phenomenon as well as the fact that there is no living thing in the Sea.

The sea is surrounded by mountains and those on the Jordanian shore are the mountains of Ammon and Moab. Here Moses first viewed the promised land *Deut 34:1-3*.

The Dead Sea

EILAT

Name
Means 'terebinth tree'.
Location
On the Red Sea at the outlet of the Araua Plain. The most southerly settlement in Israel.
Bible references
During the exodus, the tribes stayed here *Deut 2:8*. Eilat was also an important harbour in the time of Solomon *1 Kings 9:26*, *1 Kings 22:47f*.
What to see

Aquarium
This is built on the shore and through a glass window built into the sea allows a beautiful view of the corals.

Maritime Museum
Murray Centre

On the gulf of Eilat

EIN GEDI

Name
Means 'fountain of a kid'.
Location
Some caves halfway along the Israeli shore of the Dead Sea. 11 miles from Masada.

Ein Gedi, general view

Bible reference
David was fleeing from King Saul and hid in the caves *1 Sam 24:1–15*.

History
Bar Kókhba, a Jewish rebellion leader in A.D. 132, hid here.

What to do
Have a swim in an unusual spring as it tumbles out of the rocks.

EIN KAREM

Name
Means 'vineyards by the spring'.

Location
West of Jerusalem. Bus 27. About 5 miles from Central Bus Station. The village is in the hollow of terraced hills carved out by economy-minded workers centuries ago. The University Hospital of Hadassa is nearby, just off the Jerusalem–Tel Aviv road.

Ein Karem

Bible references
The village corresponds to the description in *Lk 1:39* and was near enough for Zacharias to attend the temple as a priest *Lk 1:5*. Tradition places John the Baptist's birth here *Lk 1:36*.

Mary visited here and uttered the Magnificat *Lk 1:39f, 46f*.

History
Christian tradition dates from A.D. 530 when Theodosius wrote about his pilgrimage. An ancient church festival calendar gives a day

to St Elizabeth and tells of a church at Ein Karem. Since the 10th century a church here has been dedicated to St John.

What to see

St John's Church The present building dates from 1675. Some stone can be seen from earlier Roman and Crusader churches as well as Byzantine mosaic. Descent by stone steps inside the church leads to a grotto.

The Spring of the Vineyard This is situated within a small mosque. The Crusaders venerated the spot to celebrate the visit of the Mother of Jesus.

EMMAUS

Location

There are three places that lay claim to the biblical Emmaus:

Imwas 15 miles west of Jerusalem. Jerome thought that this was the site but it is 160 furlongs, not 60 furlongs from Jerusalem. There are remains of an ancient monastery, now owned by a French concern. Note the interesting baptism cavity: adult and child side by side.

Abu Ghosh See page 7.

El Qubeibeh Near Nebi Samuel. This village has no tourist site, but can claim to be the most authentic place of Emmaus of the Bible. It is 7 miles from Jerusalem.

Bible reference

Home of Cleopas *Lk 24:13–32*. Also the resurrection appearance.

ESDRAELON, Valley of

Name
Jezreel and Esdraelon are the same in Greek and Hebrew for 'God sows'.

Location
A triangular shaped valley in Galilee west of the Jordan rift valley.

Bible references
In the plain, there are two places of biblical interest:

Megiddo Megiddo was the fortress that guarded the plain. Solomon maintained a garrison of horses and chariots, well-suited for flat-land warfare *1 Kings 4:12, 1 Kings 9:15–19*. Ahaziah died there during his flight *2 Kings 9:27*; as did Josiah *2 Chron 35:20f*.

Its strategic location brings it to the fore in the prophecy of the closing age, as Megiddo and Armageddon are related words *Zech 12:11, Rev 16:16*.

Jezreel The city of Jezreel has yet to be located but there is a kibbutz about 2 miles from Afula, bearing the same name. It was the residence of Ahab and his wicked Queen Jezebel *2 Kings 9–10*. Elijah ran before Ahab's chariot *1 Kings 18*. The name Jezreel became synonymous with judgement *Hos 1:4*.

History
The valley has always been of strategic importance. The Romans called it the Via Maris – 'the way of the sea', and before that it was called Derech Hayam – 'the road to adventure'. As far back as 1478 B.C., the

Megiddo, columns from King David's period

proud Pharaoh had carved details of his victory there onto stone.

In 1918 General Allenby broke the back of the Turkish army and in 1948 the Jews defeated the Arabs five times here, barring the road to Haifa.

About 30 years ago, it was largely marshy and overgrown with rushes. Today, the cotton plantations yield a crop five times larger per acre than in Egypt.

Megiddo

What to see

The ancient remains are full of interest and are a real must on the pilgrimage.

Look at the model at the entrance, which explains the history and layout. Explore the ruins of Solomon's stables. Look for the tunnel which brought water into the garrison in times of siege. There is also a display of Canaanite remains.

Megiddo, partial view of excavations

GALILEE, SEA OF

Sea of Galilee, Jewish fishermen

Names

Hebrew *Galil* which means 'a circle' or 'district'. The modern Hebrew name is *Yam Kinneret*, which means 'a harp', because of the lake's shape.

Location

In the north-east of Israel.

Bible references

There are two Old Testament names *Num 34:11* and *Josh 12:3*; and two New Testament ones *Lk 5:1* and *Jn 21:1*. King Solomon was generous here *1 Kings 9:11*.

Jesus called his followers to follow him here *Mk 1:16*. He calmed a storm after the experienced fishermen panicked *Mk 4:35f*. A miracle of walking on the water took place here *Mt 14:25f*.

During the time of the resurrection appearances, Jesus came to the disciples here *Jn 21*. Christians were to be found in the region from earliest times *Acts 9:31*.

A modern settlement, Ein Ger, is on the eastern shore, opposite Tiberias, and nearby is a hill called Sussilia, site of one of the 'ten towns' of Decapolis *Mk 7:31*. North of this is the site of Gadara *Mt 8:28*.

History

In Bible times, the surrounding hills were covered by trees, but the conquering Turks destroyed most of them. Because of the fertile soil and the trade route, there were ten towns dotted along the shore. The population is reputed to have reached 100,000.

Along its shores, great battles have been

Sea of Galilee, Mt Hermon in distance

fought by the Egyptians, Philistines, Romans and Crusaders, as well as Turks.

Features

This natural-water lake has always provided a livelihood from fishing and today there are modern sardine canning factories. Over 20 species of fish can be caught. Perhaps the most famous is 'Peter's fish' or Tilapia *Mt 17:24–27*. The male is able to carry the spawn in a tiny sac under the mouth. It is also known to be attracted by bright objects. It is fished at night *Jn 21:3*.

A chapel at Tabgha to the north-east of the lake, commemorates the multiplication of the loaves and fish *Mk 6:34*.

GIBEAH

Name

Means 'a hill'.

Location

Just north of Mount Scopus on the city boundary of Jerusalem, on the right, is a hill.

The guide will point to an unfinished Palace of King Hussain's. The 1967 war stopped the building of his 'show palace'.

Bible references

City north of Jerusalem *Is 10:29*. It was destroyed as a punishment *Judg 19f*. Birthplace of Saul *1 Sam 10:26, 11:4*. He lived there *1 Sam 13f*.

History

The site has been inhabited ever since water cisterns were invented. The remains show that the place did have a great fire *Judg 20:40*. Saul built a fortress here but for centuries the site was derelict until the Maccabees built another fort. Since King Hussain was forced to abandon his project, the site is still unoccupied.

What to see

The archaeological diggings show several layers from the various periods mentioned.

GOOD SAMARITAN INN

Good Samaritan Inn

Location

Halfway between Jerusalem and Jericho. In the Wilderness of Judah.

Bible references

It is thought that John the Baptist preached repentance around these parts *Mt 3*. Jesus used this well-known halfway Inn in a parable *Lk 10:34*.

What to see

From ancient times an inn has stood here. It served as a caravanserai and police post, to bring control to the surrounding desolate country. There is a well, a courtyard and the remains of a building.

The pilgrim can easily picture how welcome such a place would be for the traveller on such a dangerous and tiring road. Jesus himself travelled this way.

From your tour coach, watch out for the ancient road to Jericho alongside the modern one.

HAIFA

Location

Israel's main sea port in the north of the country.

Haifa by night

History

This is Israel's third most populous city of 225,000. The British first took advantage of the place as a natural port. For centuries before that, Jaffa had been the main trade and import/export centre.

German colonists came next and began expanding in a most orderly way. Before the British gave it a fresh start, it had been Arab, Crusader and Turkish settlements.

The inhabitants will never forget one night in 1939 when the ship 'Struma' lost all but one of its 764 passengers, seeking 'illegal' immigration, under the British mandate.

Today, it is a bustling, clean, attractive city with all the usual municipal facilities for entertainment, sightseeing and recreation.

What to see

See under *Carmel*, page 22.

HAZOR

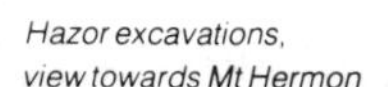

Hazor excavations, view towards Mt Hermon

Name
Means 'cattle'.
Location
15 miles north-west of Tiberius.
Bible references
In Old Testament days this was the principal northern city. Jabin was king here *Judg 4:2, 17*. The site is mentioned in ancient Assyrian and Egyptian records. Joshua conquered it *Josh 11:10, 19:36*. Solomon made it one of his chariot towns *1 Kings 9:15*. When the Assyrians invaded Israel in 732 B.C. it was one of the first cities to fall *2 Kings 15:29*.
What to see
First, have a delicious meal at the Kibbutz Restaurant and shop in the spacious and modern precinct.

Then take time to explore the extensive excavations covering many centuries of ruins. There are two distinct parts–the **Acropolis** on the highest area, and the lower city to the north.

HEBRON

Name
Hebron means 'confederacy' in Hebrew but there is an older name of Kiriath-Arba which means 'tetrapolis' or 'four cities' *Josh 14:15*.
Location
It is the highest city (3050 feet) in the Holy

Land and is approx. 19 miles south-south-west of Jerusalem. It can claim to have been inhabited for about 5000 years.

Bible references

Abraham pitched his tents nearby at Mamre *Gen 13:18, Gen 18:1*. He bought a field to bury Sarah *Gen 23:19*. David was anointed king and ruled seven years before entering Jerusalem *2 Sam 2f, 2 Sam 5:3*.

Absalom, David's son, planned to overthrow David from Hebron *2 Sam 15:7*. Exiles returned here from Babylonian captivity *Neh 11:25*.

What to see

Hebron is important to Moslems, Jews and Christians. A mosque surrounds the Cave of Machpelah and is called The Tomb of the Patriarchs. To the Moslem it is one of the four sacred cities of Islam because of Abram (the friend of God). To the Jew, it is next in importance to the Wailing Wall. To the Christian, the site is a reminder of what faith in Christ really means *Rom 4:3, Gal 3:16*.

The high wall surrounding the mosque is Herodian and is 50 feet high and 10 feet thick. A Crusader church was built during the 12th century.

Today, Jews and Moslems worship in the same building but at different times. This is unique.

Hebron

JERICHO

Name
The name could mean 'moon'.
Location
At the south end of the Jordan valley is a plain before the river Jordan enters the Dead Sea.
Bible references

Old Testament
Deut 34:3. Joshua captured the city as the walls collapsed *Josh 6:20.* Rebuilt *1 Kings 16:34.* David stayed here *2 Sam 10:5.* Elijah and Elisha both visited the city *2 Kings 2:1f.* Elisha purified the spring after an ancient prophecy had been fulfilled *Josh 6:26, 1 Kings 16:34, 2 Kings 2:18f.* Inhabitants were resettled after the captivity *Ezra 2:34.* The people went to Jerusalem to help Nehemiah *Neh 3:2.*

New Testament
Jesus healed blind Bartimaeus *Mk 10:46.* He also went with a special purpose to Zacchaeus' house *Lk 19:1f.*

History
This oasis has always had palm trees lining its streets. It is strategically placed to guard the crossing of the Jordan and has natural resources of flowing spring water. Archaeologists testify that it may have been inhabited as long ago as 10,000 B.C. Perhaps this is the oldest city in the world.

There are three definite periods, each with its remains:

Earliest Times
Tell-es-Sultan is to the west of modern Jericho, facing the 'Mount of Temptation' and just across the road from 'Elisha's fountain'. The 'tell' or mound is about

400 × 200 feet. Because of the water and trees, the place is able to support a settled community and animals were domesticated and ground was tilled. The pilgrim will see a stone tower with 20 steps, which has been uncovered. This is a very remarkable find.

Old Testament

Jericho was destroyed about 1600 B.C., probably by the Egyptians. Pottery has been found dating from about 4000 B.C. The Early Bronze Age again saw rebuilding (this was the same time as the Pyramids were built). Tombs for the same period as Abraham have revealed good-looking furniture and household implements. The major periods of building since Joshua through to Nehemiah and Herod have left few remains, probably because clay was used for building.

New Testament

Herod the Great rebuilt the city, in the west of the present city at Tulul Abu el-Alayiqi'. Its hot climate attracted the rich people from northern cities who preferred it to their cold winter period.

Jericho, market square

Jericho, site of Hisham's Palace

Jericho, Elisha's fountain

What to see

Elisha's Fountain
It is good to read the Bible account from *2 Kings 2:19*, as the pilgrims dangle their feet in the flowing stream!

Hisham's Palace
Here are the remains of a rich Damascan caliph (7th century A.D.) who lavished money on a palace, only to see it collapse four years later in an earthquake. Don't miss the beautiful mosaic called 'The Tree of Life' on the bath-house floor!

Palestinian Refugee Camps
Take note of the two derelict Palestinian Refugee camps to the north and south of the city. Before the Six Day War in 1967 they housed over 30,000 refugees, who have now mostly fled to the east bank, that is Jordan.

Because of security restrictions, the pilgrim is unable to visit the east side of Jericho where the river Jordan is. Several churches commemorate the baptism of Jesus. The river is narrower than imagined and unspectacular *2 Kings 5:12, Mk 1:10f.*

A 'sycamore' tree
Notice the tree lined roads and look for a 'sycamore tree' (*Lk 19:4*) pointed out to you by the guide.

Tell es-Sultan
At this pre-Joshua site visit the Tower. The visitor should wear a head covering because of the danger of sunburn.

JERUSALEM

Jerusalem

JERUSALEM

History

Jerusalem is a holy city to Moslems, Jews and Christians. Its history stretches back across the centuries. Abraham returned this way after a great victory, and was met by Melchizedek with offerings of bread and wine *Gen 14:18*.

David saw the potential of the terrain as a military and administrative centre and so captured it *2 Sam 5:2*. He later brought the ark of covenant into the city *2 Sam 6*. Solomon fulfilled his father's dream of building a temple *1 Kings 6*.

Nebuchadnezzar, King of Babylon, destroyed the temple in his conquest and he deported the major part of the population. This happened in 587 B.C. *2 Chron 36:17-20.*

50 years later Cyrus, King of Persia, conquered Babylon and then set about repatriating the people. Nehemiah had an interesting time while supervising the rebuilding of the walls and temple–*Neh 4*.

The year 332 B.C. saw Alexander the Great enter the city as yet another conqueror. The Maccabees led a revolt when worship foreign to Judaism was introduced into the temple. From 165 B.C. to 63 B.C. the Hasmoneans ruled the city as an independent area.

The Roman legions in their expansionist policy marched into Jerusalem soon after 63 B.C. and in 37 B.C. Herod the Great was appointed King. He was terribly cruel, but also a master builder. He rebuilt the city and extended the temple for the third time. There is much of Herod's handiwork left.

The pilgrim can read of the destruction of the city in A.D. 70 by Titus and his legionaries in the writings of Josephus, the Jewish historian. The temple was razed, the city ruined and the nation ceased to be. It was the start of the Dispersion.

From A.D. 70 to the present has been covered in most history books. The new Jerusalem of 415,000 persons has ambitions of nearly doubling its size. This city, perched 2400 feet up in the Judaean hills, is now once more the capital of Israel. It will play a decisive role in the world's history, until Christ comes again.

Jerusalem, walls of Old City

Jerusalem, Lion's Gate

The Walls

Maps show three areas of walls encircling the city at various times. Because of the steep drop into the Kidron Valley, any extension in area has always had to be in a northward direction.

One thing the pilgrim always has to remember is that the Jerusalem that Jesus knew lies buried beneath the present 'old city'. The buildings we see, the streets – including the Via Dolorosa, the walls and gates, are of a time a few centuries later.

David's city was mainly at Ophel, which faces the Kidron Valley. Nehemiah extended it westwards and Herod extended it northwards. This accounts for three separate circumferences. This also explains why the Church of the Holy Sepulchre lies within the present walls, but in the time of Christ it would have been 'outside the city wall' *Jn 19:20*.

The Gates

The ancient wall that still surrounds the city dates mostly from the time of the Turkish Sultan Suleiman the Magnificent (1538–41). There are remains of walls built by Herod from 37 B.C. It is possible to walk along the top ramparts and enjoy the excellent views. The length is approx. 2½ miles and there are seven open gates.

Do not walk in the heat of the day.

Zion Gate

Also known as 'David's Gate' by the Arabs.

Before the 1948 war, it was used by Moslem pilgrims to the traditional tomb of

David. After the 1967 Six Day War the gate was repaired.

Dung Gate Since Nehemiah's time, refuse was carried out of the city via only one gate.

Lion's Gate So named because of the lions carved above the gate. Also known as St Stephen's Gate and Mary's Gate. It leads into the Via Dolorosa.

Israeli paratroopers broke through here during the 1967 conflict.

Herod's Gate So named because medieval pilgrims looked erroneously for the house of Herod Antipas nearby. Moslems think that people will assemble here before the Day of Judgement.

Damascus Gate Faces the northern city of Shechem and is the start of the Damascus Road. Through an earlier gate on this exact site, Saul started his 'journey to a new life' *Acts 9*. See also *Solomon's Quarries*, page 59, *Garden Tomb*, page 57.

New Gate Only opened in 1887 – hence its name. It functioned as an access to new suburbs beyond the city, as Jews began to migrate back to the Holy Land.

Jaffa Gate Also known as Bab el Khatil ('gate of friend') because of an Arabic inscription 'There is no god but Allah and Abraham is his friend'. A moat was filled in during the visit of Kaiser Wilhelm II in 1898, allowing a mounted procession to enter the old city. See also *Christ Church*, page 57.

Antonia Fortress

Location

Remaining wall is in the north-west corner of the temple compound.

Bible references
Jesus was held here *Mk 15:16*. The soldiers rushed to Paul *Acts 21:32–40*.
History
Built by Herod in honour of his friend Mark Anthony, it served as a garrison to watch over the temple activities.

Bethesda Pool

Jerusalem, Bethesda Pool

Location
Within the compound of St Anne's Church on Al Mwahideen Street.
Bible references
Jesus miraculously cured a cripple *Jn 5:2*.
What to see
The excavated area of the pool, surrounded by remains of several churches.

The Church of the Holy Sepulchre

Location
At the corner of Et Takieh and Khan Ez-Zeit Streets.
Bible references
This lays claim to be the authentic site of Golgotha and the tomb *Jn 19:17, 41*.
History
Queen Helena, Emperor Constantine's mother, identified the site in A.D. 326 as being under a Roman temple to Venus. A church was then built and this stood until 614 when the Persians destroyed it. In 1149 the first of several further buildings were built.

The Citadel

Jerusalem, The Citadel

Location

Overlooking the Jaffa Gate.

Bible references

Since Crusader times, it has been wrongly titled 'David's Tower', referring to his adulterous sin with Bathsheba *2 Sam 11:2*. However, Jesus saw and knew the place as a garrison for the 10th Roman Legion. He would have entered the Citadel on his way to meet with Herod Antipas who was in residence *Lk 23:7*.

History

Built by Herod the Great, the Citadel is one of the prominent landmarks in the city. It was protected by three towers called Phasael, Hippicus and Marianne. Phasael was Herod's brother, and the base of this tower is still standing. The name Hippicus continues to be a mystery because he was an unknown friend of the King. The Queen was Marianne whom he loved passionately but nevertheless condemned her to death!

The Crusaders rebuilt the Citadel but most of the present excavations reveal rebuilding by the Turkish Sultan Suleiman the Magnificent in 1540. The minaret was built in 1665. It was from here that General Allenby declared British rule in 1917. From 1948-67 it was occupied by the Jordanian Arab Legion.

Let us remember one thing: this is the only building in Jerusalem that has been left standing from the time of Christ.

See also page 61.

Mount Moriah, the temple with the Dome of the Rock

Jerusalem, Dome of the Rock

Name

'Haram esh-Sherif'

Bible references

Abraham brought his son Isaac with the intention of sacrifice *Gen 22:2*. David bought the site *2 Sam 24:18f*. The first temple was built by Solomon *2 Chron 3*. (The vision of Ezekiel is an elaboration of this *Ezek 40f.*) It was destroyed by Nebuchad-nezzar in 587 B.C. The second temple was built by returning exiles and was authorized by Cyrus *Ezra 3f*. The third temple was built by Herod but its prime purpose was not the worship of God, but as a prestigious piece of public relations by the half-Jewish king *Mk 13:1*, *Lk 13:31f*, *Acts 3:11*.

It was begun in about 19 B.C. and destroyed in A.D. 70, by fire, *Mt 24:1,2*.

History

In A.D. 135, the Romans built a temple to Jupiter on the site and the Moslem caliph Abdel Malik built the mosque in A.D. 687. During the Crusader period, it became the Church of the Order of Templars.

The Dome was restored in 1959. The magnificent carpets in the Dome were a gift by the King of Morocco.

What to see

The esplanade surrounding the Dome has several features of interest, each of which will be pointed out by your guide.

The Dome of Ascension This is a copy of the Byzantine dome on the Mount of Olives. It commemorated the supposed leap by Mohammed into heaven.

Dome of the Chain This was once used to store silver.

The El Aksa Mosque This is Islam's holiest shrine after Mecca and Medina. It has special significance to freemasons because it has historical connections to Solomon's palace.

The El Kas fountain It is used by Moslems for ritual washings before their prayer times.

The Golden Gate This is now walled up. Jesus may have entered the city here on Palm Sunday.

The Islam Museum There is a collection of Byzantine and Islamic excavated findings.

Solomon's Stables These are huge vaults underneath the south-east corner of the temple area. They were built by Herod to support the temple platform. There is no evidence that they were part of Solomon's stables of 40,000 horses *1 Kings 4:26*.

The Summer Pulpit This was erected in 1456.

Robinson's Arch

This is a projection on the southern corner of the Wailing Wall. Discovered in 1838. A series of steps from road level to the temple.

Via Dolorosa

Name
'The Way of the Cross'. It is a Roman Catholic devotional exercise.

Location
Within the old city, starting at the Antonia Fortress to Golgotha. The events of this last journey of Jesus are portrayed by 14 stations.

The 14 stations are:

Bible references

1 The condemnation by Pontius Pilate *Mt 27:26*.
2 Jesus receives the cross, *Mk 15:20*.
3 Jesus falls. A tradition.
4 Mary meets Jesus. A tradition.
5 Simon of Cyrene is forced to carry the cross *Lk 23:26*.
6 Veronica wipes Jesus' face. A tradition.
7 Jesus falls. A tradition.
8 Jesus speaks to the women *Lk 23:27f*.
9 Jesus falls. A tradition.
10 Jesus is stripped *Jn 19:23*.
11 The nails are driven in *Mt 27:35*, *Mk 15:25*.
12 Jesus dies *Mk 15:37*, *Lk 23:49*.
13 Jesus' body is taken down *Lk 23:53*.
14 Jesus is laid in the tomb *Jn 19:38f*.

Jerusalem, Lithostrotos

What to see
Interesting places visited during the devotional exercise include the Sisters of Zion Convent, where the pilgrim can see the Lithostrotos (or 'Pavement' *Jn 19:13*) which shows genuine marks from the Roman

Jerusalem, Via Dolorosa

period, the 'Ecce Homo' Arch built in A.D. 135, a Polish Chapel and Museum at Station 3, and the Church of the Holy Sepulchre (see page 43).

Further tips

Spend time around the area of the Sisters of Zion. The pilgrim is recommended to purchase a full colour leaflet called Amirs Guide Yourself Guide from the little bookshop within the Convent. Ask for the English-speaking Sister to give a guided tour.

If you wish to explore the area at leisure and therefore do not wish to join the crowds each Friday on the processional route, you will be able to see the Museum at the Convent and the Museum at the Polish Chapel (ask the attendant if you can hold a little oil lamp). You can also take your time exploring the Church of the Holy Sepulchre with the aid of a free map from any tourist centre.

Do not be waylaid by street salesmen selling religious curios or soft drinks. Very few offer genuine quality goods and in any case following in the footsteps of Jesus is hardly the time for compulsive purchases!

The Western (Wailing) Wall

The Western Wall was built as part of the Temple extension of Herod. In A.D. 70, Titus razed the temple and toppled parts of the outer wall. These huge blocks of stone are the remains of the base of the wall. What Herod built, he built strong.

The Jews venerate the wall because it stood nearest to the temple which was

Jerusalem, The Western (Wailing) Wall

defiled by the Roman soldiers. They come to bewail the loss of the temple. The crying and weeping gave rise to another name – the 'Wailing Wall'.

Wilson's Arch

Within a tunnel to the left of the Western Wall. It was discovered by an Army Officer in the last century. It is a section of a bridge which connected the temple with the upper city.

JERUSALEM – Kidron Valley

Jerusalem, Kidron Valley

Location

The valley, east of the temple mount, between Jerusalem and the Mount of Olives. It meets the Hinnom valley in the south.

What to see

Absalom's Pillar

This is the inverted-cone shaped pillar. The tomb chamber dates from several centuries later than Absalom's death *2 Sam 18:18*. Jesus would have passed by, and the Christian remembers that Absalom was the disloyal royal son but Jesus was the loyal Son of God *2 Sam 15:10*, *Mt 26:39*.

The other two tombs are supposed to be of the sons of Hezir and of Zecharius.

The Gihon Spring

This was one of Jerusalem's earliest water supplies, it is over 3000 years old *1 Kings 1:33, 38, 45*.

Hezekiah's Tunnel Because the Gihon was outside the city wall, Hezekiah channelled the water into Siloam (716 B.C.). It was a wonderful feat of engineering because the diggers started from both ends and met in the middle, a distance of 600 yards through solid rock *2 Chron 32:30, 2 Kings 20:20.*

Pool of Siloam Here Jesus cured a blind man *Jn 9:11*.

St Peter in Gallicantu Church This commemorates Peter's denial *Lk 22:54f*. Here is one of the authentic remains. There is an ancient stone pathway which Jesus undoubtedly would have used in his entrance into the city, from the Mount of Olives *Jn 18:12*. The official residences were on this side of the city.

Tombs There are three distinct ones, although there are numerous others. Jews and Moslems value being buried near sacred places. Jews think that the Last Judgement will begin here *Joel 3:12*.

Jerusalem, steps up from Kidron Valley

What to see

Basilica of the Agony
This is also called 'All Nations Church'. It is very beautiful and a distinctive feature is its 12 cupolas. The pilgrim is shown a 'Rock of Agony' *Lk 22:44*.

Bethphage
A tiny village on the eastern slope. The Palm Sunday procession started here *Lk 19:29*. See also page 17.

Dome of Ascension
A traditional site to mark Christ's ascension, dating from A.D. 380. The small chapel is bounded by an octagonal wall. This building inspired the architecture for the Dome of the Rock *Mk 16:19*.

Dominus Flevit
There are archaeological remains of a wine press, cistern and mosaic of a Byzantine monastery. The beautiful tear-shaped chapel commemorates Jesus weeping over Jerusalem *Lk 19:41*.

Jerusalem, Dominus Flevit Chapel

Jerusalem,
Garden of Gethsemane

The Garden of Gethsemane This small garden contains eight ancient olive trees. Because olive renews itself, it is probably true that these present trees are shoots of the ones standing in Bible times *Mt 26:36*.

Jewish Cemetery This is on the Mount of Olives facing Jerusalem. It is one of Judaism's oldest cemeteries. It is sacred because of the prophecy concerning judgement and resurrection *Joel 3:2,14.* The tradition for using the site as a burial ground began with Absalom *2 Sam 18:18.*

Pater-Noster Church This is one of the earliest Christian places of devotion, erected in 333 by Queen Helena.

It marks where Jesus spoke to his disciples about Jerusalem *Mt 24–25*, *Lk 11:1–4*.

Tower of Ascension This is the tallest church on the Mount. It is a Russian Orthodox church and from the top of the tower magnificent views are possible.

There is also a Greek and Russian Orthodox church. A traditional burial site for Mary the Mother of Jesus can also be seen.

Jerusalem, Mount Zion

Name

Mount Zion is the Old Testament name for one of the hills of Jerusalem and was an alternative name for David's City.

Bible reference

Ps 48 tells of Zion being elevated because of its part in the defence of Jerusalem. God is stronger than a mountain.

What to see

The Basilica of the Dormiton

This is a beautiful church with a long history. Especially remarkable is the circular mosaic floor. Since the 7th century a tradition has linked the site with Mary's death.

Cellar of the Holocaust

This is a building dedicated to the 6 million Jews murdered in the Second World War. This is well worth a visit for two reasons.

The first is to remember, and grieve and ask for forgiveness; the second is to notice the Jewish customs associated with the shrine.

The Cenacle

This is another medieval site dating from A.D. 1335, supposedly marking the site of the Last Supper *Lk 22:14f*. About the 5th century, another tradition began linking the site with Pentecost *Acts 2:4*. But the structure is nothing like that of an ancient 'upper room'.

What is true, however, is that the earliest Christians met on Mount Zion because of the prophecy of Isaiah *Is 2:3*.

David's Tomb

This is within a medieval building without architectural merit. It is a traditional spot since the visit of Rabbi Benjamin of the 12th century. This richly decorated tomb is venerated by Jews, but cannot really be David's tomb *1 Kings 2:10*.

The Valley of Hinnom

This is the valley that Mount Zion overlooks. It was the boundary between the tribes of Judah and Benjamin. It has sad associations: Kings Ahaz and Manasseh offered

Jerusalem, Valley of Hinnom

worship to a false god and part of the ritual was forcing children through fire *2 Chron 28:3, 2 Chron 33:6*. Josiah condemned the place *2 Kings 23:10*.

Not far away, on the southern slope, is 'Akeldama'–the field of blood *Acts 1:18, 19*. This refuse tip that always smouldered with the city's rubbish was equated by Jesus with a type of hell *Mk 9:47, 48*.

JERUSALEM–New City

What to see

Hadassah Hospital

This hospital was founded by an American Jewess in 1912. Based in West Jerusalem, it is the largest hospital in Israel. Within the hospital is a modern synagogue with twelve stained-glass windows, depicting the twelve tribes of Israel. They were made by the world famous artist, Marc Chagall, and are well worth a visit.

Jerusalem, Hadassah Hospital Chagall windows

The Knesset

The Hebrew *Knesset*, like the Greek *synagogue*, means 'meeting place' or 'gathering'. This is the Israeli parliament; the building is very modern.

It is interesting to think that there have been four forms of government in Israel:

by 'able men' *Ex 18:14f.*
by judges *Judg 12:8f.*
by kings *Judg 21:25*, *1 Sam 8:6*.
by governors *Neh 5:14*, *Mt 27:2*.

The Menora

This seven branched candelabrum stands opposite the main entrance to the Knesset. It is a gift of the British Parliament and shows scenes from Israelite history.

Candlesticks are mentioned a lot in the Bible: A lampstand was part of the tabernacle furniture *Ex 25:31*; ten were provided for Solomon's temple *1 Kings 7:49*; Christ walks between the lampstands *Rev 2:1*; heaven itself is lit by Christ *Rev 21:23*.

Jerusalem, The Menora at night with Knesset in background

The Yad Vashem Monument

This commemorated the 6 million European Jews who were murdered by the Nazis. There is an avenue of trees planted by non-Jews who risked their lives to aid escaping Jews. A flame flickers in memory of those who died.

Despite an attempt at extermination, the nation lives on. *Deut 7:6–11* is very appropriate.

JERUSALEM – Other places of interest

Christ Church

Location
Just inside Jaffa Gate.

Features
This is the oldest Anglican church in the Holy Land and was consecrated in 1849. The first Anglican bishop in Jerusalem was a converted Rabbi. The site is of interest because it contains foundations of Herod the Great's palace *Lk 23:7*. Christ Church has an evangelical tradition and regular services are held. Note the Ten Commandments in Hebrew on the reredos. There is a hostel within the compound.

The Garden Tomb

About 300 yards from the Damascus Gate up the Nablus road is the Garden Tomb. It is

Jerusalem, The Garden Tomb

Jerusalem, Golgotha (possible site)

administered by evangelical Christians. A Sunday morning service is held, for visitors and local Christians. It is a lovely place for quiet.

When the property was acquired in 1894, a society was formed 'for the preservation of the tomb and garden outside the walls of Jerusalem, believed by many people to be the Sepulchre and garden of Joseph of Arimathaea'. The society was 'instituted so that the Garden Tomb, Jerusalem, may be kept sacred as a quiet spot and preserved from desecration'.

In the Garden are trees, shrubs and flowers typical of Bible times, and its very naturalness has helped thousands to visualize the events of the first Easter Day and to experience the presence of our risen Lord in an atmosphere of faith and worship *Jn 20:11, 15*. Sunday morning worship is at 9a.m. Christian groups may hold a Communion Service by prior arrangement.

Mea Shearim

This is where the orthodox Jews live–people who still today try to live a strictly religious way of life. The area was built in 1875 by European Jews trying to defend themselves from Arab raiders: the name *mea shearim* means '100 gateways' *Gen 26:12*.

It is a fascinating place to visit but the pilgrim is respectfully asked to dress modestly and not to drive through the area during the Sabbath.

Mount Scopus

Situated as a vantage point (*skopos* is Greek for 'watch') to the east and south, it has always been a strategic military target.

On the mount are the ultra-modern Hebrew University, Hadassah Hospital, the War Cemetery and the Truman Research Centre.

Solomon's Quarries

Location

Under the City Wall, adjacent to the Damascus Gate.

Jerusalem, Solomon's Quarries

Bible references
In order to get the stone to build the first temple and surrounding buildings, Solomon had forced labour quarry *1 Kings 5:15*. The sound of quarrying could not be heard at the temple site *1 Kings 6:7*. Well worth a visit.

Tombs of the Kings

Location
Nablus Road.

Features
A wealthy queen called Helena of Adiabene embraced Judaism in 54 B.C. These are her family's tombs. Of interest is the extra-ordinary work put into a perpetual memorial, digging a flight of 25 steps out of solid rock. Note also a 'rolled tomb stone'.

Jerusalem, model of the second Temple (see Holy Land Hotel, page 62)

Churches

Baptist Southern Worship Rasheed Street.

Baraka Bible Church Presbyterian. Hebron Road (Bethlehem).

Christ Church Evangelical. Jaffa Gate.

Church of the Nazarene International Centre. 33 Nablus Road.

Church of the Redeemer Lutheran. Muristan Street.

First Baptist Bible Church Saladin Street.

Garden Tomb Interdenominational. Nablus Road and Derech Scheuhem Road. Regular Sunday morning service. Bible-based ministry.

The Holy Sepulchre Roman Catholic. Old City.

St George's Cathedral Anglican/Episcopal. Nablus Road and Saladin Street.

Museums

Agricultural Museum Helena Hamalka Street. Sundays to Fridays 8 a.m. to 1 p.m.

Ancient agricultural tools, some of which are 2000 years old.

Biblical Zoo Catch bus 15 near junction of Yirmiyahu and Shanger Streets. Animals, birds and reptiles mentioned in the Bible are on view. Each animal has its appropriate biblical text on display.

The Citadel Adjacent to Jaffa Gate. Sundays to Thursdays 8 a.m. to 7 p.m., Fridays 8 a.m. to 4 p.m. A Son et Lumière (sound and light drama) takes place here nightly throughout the tourist season, April to October in

English 8.45p.m. except Fridays. It depicts the history of Israel seen through the uses of one stone found during archaeological diggings. This is a real must of a visit and the pilgrim is advised to dress warmly.

Inside the Citadel's walls, there is the Jerusalem City Museum. There is an audio-visual presentation of the history of the site of Jerusalem. Again, this is a must for the pilgrim to visit. The programme is shown in English at 9a.m., 11a.m., 1p.m. and 3p.m.

Holy Land Hotel

Within the grounds of this hotel there is a 1/50th scale model of Jerusalem in Jesus' day. Open daily from 8.30a.m. – 5.30p.m. and Fridays from 9a.m. – 12p.m.

A visit here at the start of the pilgrimage ensures the Bible reader of a good view of the events of Holy Week and other Bible incidents.

Israel Museum

Really four museums in one. Within walking distance from the Knesset.

As well as housing Israel's main Museum of Art and Folklore, the Bible reader will want to spend most time in the Shrine of the Book

Jerusalem, Israel Museum Shrine of the Book

which has the Dead Sea Scrolls and relics on view. The Shrine preserves in its underground vaults the Dead Sea Scrolls discovered (1948) in the northern Wilderness of Judah, east of Jerusalem, and ancient manuscripts found in the southern part of the Wilderness of Judah and in the excavations of Mount Masada on the shore of the Dead Sea.

The architecture of the Shrine of the Book is symbolical of an inverted cave, the roof resembling the lid of a jar in which the scrolls were found. The architecture is also designed to reflect the theme of the scrolls – the conflict between the sons of light and the sons of darkness.

Open Sundays, Mondays, Wednesdays, Thursdays 10 a.m. – 5 p.m., Tuesdays 4 p.m. – 10 p.m., Saturdays 10 a.m. – 2 p.m.

Musical Instruments Museum The Rubin Academy of Smolenskin Street. Ancient and modern instruments are on view. Sunday to Friday 10 a.m. to 1 p.m.

Rockefeller Museum Salah-ed-Din Street, opposite Herod's Gate. Daily 10 a.m. – 6 p.m.

The Museum has an excellent collection of archaeological finds.

Taxation Museum 32 Agron Street.

Only the second of its kind in the world. Exhibition of methods of taxation and collection from Bible times up to the present. Well worth a visit. Sundays, Tuesdays and Thursdays between 1 and 4 p.m. Phone 28191 for appointment.

For further tourist information, see page 88.

JOPPA

Name

Yaffo means 'beautiful'.

Location

On the Mediterranean coast, 3 miles south from the centre of Tel Aviv. It served as the seaport of Jerusalem. Nowadays, it is a suburb of Tel Aviv.

Bible references

The territory around Joppa was given to the tribe of Dan *Josh 19:46*. Jonah began running away from God's call to spread his word to Gentiles *Jon 1:3*. It was also the place where the giving of the gospel to the Gentiles really began. Peter had his vision there *Acts 10:1–23*. So we can see it as a place of disobedience and obedience.

What to see

Notice the flat-roofed houses; the Flea Market, off Aleystron Street; a light-house; the Monastery of St Peter and the mythological 'Andromeda's Rock', which tells of Perseus saving Andromeda from a sea monster. The Jaffa Development Project is aiming at restoring alleys and courtyards to their appearance of 100 years ago. Nowadays antique shops and artists' galleries abound.

Joppa

River Jordan

Name
The Hebrew is *yarden* which means 'the descenders'.

Location
It is a rift valley that stretches over 160 miles, from north of Lake Huleh to the Dead Sea and beyond.

Bible references
Heavy rains fall *Josh 3:15*. Lions once roamed in this area *Jer 49:19*. The river was militarily important *Judg 12:5*. Naaman knew that it was a muddy river *2 Kings 5*.

Features
The river stems from the fort of Mount Heron in the north and into Lake Huleh which is 6 feet above sea level. It flows into Lake Galilee, 10 miles downstream. By the time the Dead Sea is reached it has descended by about 1500 feet. There are occasional hot springs which reveal its volcanic past.

KIBBUTZ

A kibbutz is a communal agricultural village. All the property is owned and managed in common by all responsible members.

Kibbutzim vary in size from about two people to some of over 1000, but the average population is between 200 and 400. The first kibbutz, called Degania, was started in 1910, and there are now over 200 kibbutzim. About 3% of Israel's population live in kibbutzim.

The kibbutz is run on simple democratic lines. The sovereign body is the 'kibbutz general meeting' which is held weekly. All members are expected to attend, participate and vote. Some sub-committees are elected.

Very many Israeli public leaders, army officers and members of the Knesset have been and continue to be members of kibbutzim.

Although the kibbutz isn't a return to a 'tribal system' its emphasis on the 'extended family' is a good grounding for national Zionist unity.

A kibbutz

View from top of Masada

Location
Between Ein Gedi and Arad, adjacent to the southern end of the Dead Sea.

History
This is a thrilling place to visit and gives valuable insight into the background history of Bible events.

Perched 1300 feet high is a plateau 1000 × 2000 feet, built on by Herod as a sumptuous palace and to hold a garrison of troops. During the Jewish uprising, Zealots (the nationalists of the day) held out here for three years against the Roman legions before taking their own lives in the face of defeat.

Josephus Flavius, the Jewish historian, wrote:

Masada

It is said that Herod prepared this fortress as a refuge in time of need against two dangers which he always envisaged: the one, that the Jewish people might depose him and put a king from the royal house which had reigned before him on the throne; and the second, even worse than the first, the fear of Cleopatra, Queen of Egypt.

This place is one of the main tourist attractions today and is reached by cable car. Be sure to bring home the attractive, informative booklet that can be purchased at the kiosk. Here you will experience wonderful panoramic views and see history at close hand.

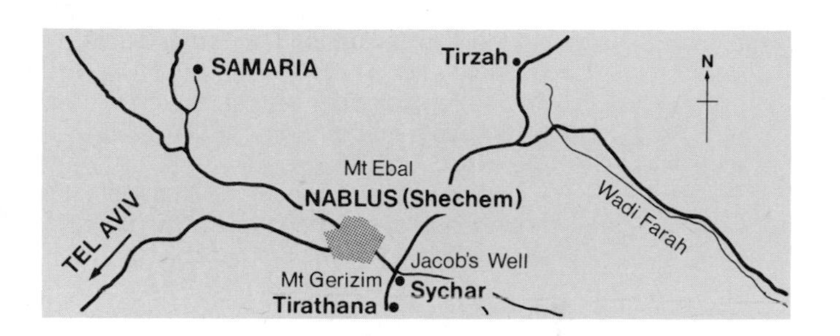

Location
30 miles north of Jerusalem.

Bible references
There are several places near this thriving Arab town on the West Bank, that has been in Jewish hands since the Six Day War, but is administered by Arab officials.

Jacob's Well
Situated just off an important crossroads where the tracks from Jerusalem and the Jordan meet. It is one of the most authentic biblical sites. The site fits exactly the two descriptions *Gen 33:18*, *Jn 4:5f*.

The well is over 150 feet deep and an unfinished Greek Orthodox church stands over the site.

Mount Ebal
(3077 feet above sea level; 1400 feet high) is still barren, in contrast to Gerizim. It is sparsely inhabited and there is no water available *Deut 11:29*.

Mount Gerizim
This still witnesses Samaritan worship *Jn 4:20*, each Passover time, as days of festivity are spent.

Samaria Modern name *Sebastia*. 7 miles from Nablus. Samaria was the capital city of the north. It stands on a 300-foot high hill, bought by Omri (885 B.C.) *1 Kings 16:24*. It became a rich city *1 Kings 22:39*, *1 Kings 20:34*. It was also considered as a centre for idolatrous worship *1 Kings 18.22*, *2 Kings 3,2*, *Is 8:4*, *Hos 7:1*.

Look over the 12th-century Crusader church built over a mosque, said to contain the tombs of Elisha and Obadiah.

The Samaritans evolved from the Israelites who were left behind during the Assyrian exile (722 B.C.) and other peoples living there *2 Kings 17:24f*. They held to the five books of Moses as their rule, 'the Mosaic Law'.

When the Jews returned from exile, they considered the Samaritans to be mixed blood and heretical and so a long-lasting feud began *Neh 4:1–2*. Jews would sooner walk three extra days and go along the Jordan whilst travelling from north to south, rather than go through Samaritan territory. Jesus was an exception *Jn 4: 3, 4, 43, Lk 10:25f*.

A visit to the Samaritans' synagogue in Nablus is worthwhile. The pilgrim need not agree with the claim that their ancient Torah comes from Joshua's time; it can only be a few centuries old.

Nowadays there are only about 500 Samaritans and they live on Mount Gerizim, and in Nablus. Intermarriage has led to difficulties.

Shechem

Just south of Nablus is the Arab village of Balata where remains of Shechem can be seen. The site is between Mount Gerizim and Ebal.

Abraham camped there *Gen 12:7*. Joseph looked for his brother nearby *Gen 37:12*. Moses informed the people *Deut 11:29* and Joshua obeyed *Josh 8.30f*. Jeroboam made the city his capital *1 Kings 12*.

Walls of Shechem

Nazareth

NAZARETH

Location

In Galilee, amidst a basin of limestone hills. It was just off the trans-continental trade routes.

Bible references

There is no mention of the town in the Old Testament. After the death of Herod, Mary and Joseph once more settled here *Mt 2:23*. Jesus had a normal upbringing and worked as a carpenter, and worshipped in the synagogue. The people of the town knew him well *Lk 4:16–31*. Jesus was known as 'Jesus of Nazareth' *Jn 1:45, 46*.

What to see

This is a town of 45,000 and is the largest Arab town in Israel. There is a new Jewish sector called Nazareth Heights and the old city is still very old-fashioned in character.

The Basilica of the Annunciation

This was built in 1965 by Roman Catholics and was funded by Catholics from all over the world. It is the largest church in the Middle East and is strikingly modern yet blends in well with the ancient atmosphere. Several caves are shown, some of which could be remains of houses from the time of Christ. The actual site remains uncertain and is not important in itself; what really matters is the fact of the incarnation: 'the word was made flesh' *Jn 1:14*.

Nazareth, Basilica of the Annunciation

The Christian Hospital

TEAR Fund helps here.

'Mary's Well'

Traditionally, this well is the one Mary used.

NEBI SAMWIL

Name
The name means 'the prophet Samuel'.

Location
A hill just outside Jerusalem on the road to Samaria. A mosque is the focal point.

Bible reference
1 Sam 28:3 contradicts the tradition that Samuel was buried here.

What to see
From the mosque vantage point, it is possible to see both the Mediterranean and the Dead Sea on a clear day. The pilgrims in ancient times first viewed Jerusalem from here. Well worth a visit, just for the view.

Qumran, caves

Location
On the west shore of the Dead Sea. It is administered by the National Parks Authority.

Significance
In 1947 the Dead Sea Scrolls were found by an Arab who was looking for a stray sheep. He threw a stone into the cave to disturb the sheep, if it were there. Instead of a bleat, there was a sound of broken pottery. Since then, archaeologists have discovered more than 500 scrolls. See also pages 62-63.

Here, surrounding the wadi, the excavations reveal a settlement of the Essenes. They were a sect within Judaism, committed to a life of piety and communal life. They tried to live strictly according to the law. The site dates from the 2nd century B.C. Their 'manual of discipline' informs us about their ideas concerning repentance, religious meals and conflicts between evil and good called 'light and darkness'.

The Isaiah scroll, perhaps the most famous one found, gives us a copy of the prophecy from the century before Christ. Indeed, the scrolls confirm the accuracy of our present Bible.

Qumran, excavations

RAMALLAH

Name

Ramallah is 'height of God' in Arabic. The biblical name is *Beth-El*, which means 'house of God'.

Location

12 miles north of Jerusalem. It is here that the traveller needs to turn right towards the village of Beitin–ancient Beth–El. The two villages are adjacent.

Bible references

Abraham offered worship *Gen 12:8*. Jacob dreamed of a ladder to God *Gen 28:10*. It was in the territory of Ephraim *1 Chron 7:28*. The ark rested there *Judg 20:26-27*. Samuel revisited it on his circuit tour *1 Sam 7:16f.* It was a centre of cultism *2 Kings 2:3, Amos 4:4.* Bethel is in fact mentioned more times in the Bible than any other place name.

Ramallah, boy's orphanage

SINAI, MOUNT

Location

The Sinai peninsula is a 360-mile triangle which joins the Gulf of Suez. Granite peaks rise 8000 feet. There is much to see and perhaps a 3–4 day visit would be wise.

Bible references

Within this triangle, the exodus wanderings took place.

The oasis Firan may be Rephidim *Ex 17:8f.* Within St Catherine's Monastery is a small room which the monks report to be the place of the burning bush *Ex 3:3f.*

Mount Sinai (7362 feet) was where Moses received the Ten Commandments *Ex 19f.*

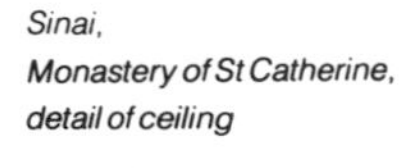

Sinai,
Monastery of St Catherine,
detail of ceiling

What to see

Monastery of St Catherine

One of the oldest monasteries in the world, it is dedicated to an Egyptian Christian martyred in the 4th century. The building itself dates from the 6th century. The church is built on the site of the burning bush. The mosque was built in the 11th century.

There is a fine collection of icons and vestments. The library is the oldest in the world and an invaluable collection of Greek, Syriac and Arabic manuscripts are still kept there. It was here that the 3rd-century Codex Sinaiticus was kept until the Russian government sold it to the British government for half a million dollars in 1933.

Sinai, Monastery of St Catherine, wood panels 17th century

TABOR, MOUNT

Location

14 miles from Nazareth, in the Jezreel valley, 1843 feet high.

Bible references

The mountain marked the boundary for the tribe of Issachar *Josh 19:17f*. From this region, Deborah and Barak recruited forces *Judg 4:6*, *Judg 5:15*. Samuel advised Saul from here *1 Sam 10:3*.

Since the 6th century, tradition has it that this is the site of the transfiguration although the name of the mountain is not given *Mt 17:1–8*.

What to see

On your ascent around the hairpin bends, look out for the great variety of trees and bushes. There is a magnificent view from the top *Ps 89:12*.

Within the Basilica are remains of Byzantine and Crusader churches.

The Jews of Galilee fortified themselves here during the revolt against the Romans in A.D. 66.

Mount Tabor

Tel Aviv

Location

A city of 1·2 million on the coast. It is the largest city in Israel. This is the nearest city to Ben Gurion airport, the Israeli international airport. Herzliya is a suburb where there are good hotels.

What to see

Carmel Market

Also called Souk, near Allenby Road/Mangen David Square. It seems as if everything is on sale here and it is a truly exciting multi-national market.

Haganah Museum This is in Rothschild Blyd. It is a permanent exhibition of the history of Israel's army, from the days in the 1930s when it trained in secret, through the immigrant smuggling days, right up to the present. Open 9 a.m. – 3 p.m.

Mann Auditorium Huberman Street. Here the Israeli Philharmonic Orchestra performs. It ranks amongst the top three orchestras in the world.

The National Opera Allenby Street. This is Israel's biggest opera house.

Shalom Sotre Achad Ha'am Street. This is Israel's big department store. At the top of this 30-storey building is an observatory which is open 10 a.m. – 10 p.m.

Haaretz Museum Ramat Aviv. Eleven museums in one. 10 a.m. – 1 p.m.

Musuem of the Jewish Diaspora Rehov Klausner. Permanent thematic exhibits showing Jewish life. Multi-media presentations. 10 a.m. – 5 p.m.

The Herodium, the unique cone-shaped fortress built to the south-east of Bethlehem by Herod the Great between 24 and 15 BC *(see page 16)*

TIBERIAS

Location
On the west coast of the Sea of Galilee.
Bible reference
Some boats came from Tiberias, bringing people that witnessed the feeding of the 5000 *Jn 6:23*.
History
There is no record of Jesus ever visiting the town. It was one of the then towns dotted along the coastline. Founded by Herod Antipas–the Herod of *Lk 3:1* in honour of the Emperor. Because it was built over a cemetery, it was not popular with Jews and so it was a mainly gentile city.

Here, the Jewish Mishna was compiled in the 2nd century A.D. Today, Tiberias has a thriving tourist industry.
What to see
The Y.M.C.A. own a beautiful chapel overlooking the lake.

Tiberias, fish market

THE MIRACLES OF JESUS

Two blind men cured	*Mt 9:27*
Demon cast out	*Mt 9:32*
Taxes provided	*Mt 17:24*
Deaf and dumb man cured	*Mk 7:31*
Blind man's sight restored	*Mk 8:22*
Jesus escapes	*Lk 4:30*
The catch of fish	*Lk 5:1*
Widow's son raised	*Lk 7:11*
Woman cured	*Lk 13:10*
Man cured	*Lk 14:1*
Ten lepers cleansed	*Lk 17:11*
Ear healed	*Lk 22:50*
Water into wine	*Jn 2:1*
Official's son cured	*Jn 4:46*
Paralysed man cured	*Jn 5:1*
Man born blind cured	*Jn 9:1*
Raising of Lazarus	*Jn 11:38*
Catch of fish	*Jn 21:1*
Woman's daughter cured	*Mk 7:24*
Feeding of 4000	*Mk 8:1*
Fig tree withered	*Mk 11:12*
Centurion's servant healed	*Mt 8:5*
Blind and dumb demoniac	*Mt 12:22*
Man with an unclean spirit	*Mk 1:21*
Peter's mother-in-law cured	*Mk 1:29*
Storm stilled on Galilee	*Mk 4:35*
Leper cured	*Mk 1:40*
Jairus' daughter raised	*Mk 5:22*
Woman's haemorrhage cured	*Mk 5:25*
Paralytic cured	*Mk 2:1*
Withered hand cured	*Mk 3:1*
Demons cast out	*Mk 9:14*
Walk on the water	*Mk 6:45*
Feeding of the 5000	*Mk 6:30*

At his baptism	*Lk 3:21*
In a lonely place	*Mk 1:35*
In the wilderness	*Lk 5:16*
Before choosing the 12	*Lk 6:12*
Before the invitation 'come unto me'	*Mt 11:25*
At the feeding of the 5000	*Jn 6:11*
After the feeding of the 5000	*Mt 14:23*
When he gave the Lord's Prayer	*Lk 11.1*
At Caesarea Philippi	*Lk 9:18*
Before his transfiguration	*Lk 9:28*
For little children	*Mt 19:13*
In the temple	*Jn 12:27*
At the Last Supper	*Mt 26:26*
For Peter	*Lk 22:32*
For the disciples	*Jn 17*
In Gethsemane	*Mt 26:36, 39, 42*
On the cross	*Lk 23:46*
At Emmaus	*Lk 24:30*

The traditional site of Jesus' temptation in the wilderness is at this mountain overlooking the Jericho valley

THE PARABLES OF JESUS

Weeds	*Mt 13:24*
Hidden treasure	*Mt 13:44*
Pearl of value	*Mt 13:45*
Net	*Mt 13:47*
Wicked servant	*Mt 18:23*
Labourer in the vineyard	*Mt 20:1*
Two sons	*Mt 21:28*
Marriage feast	*Mt 22:1*
Wise and foolish girls	*Mt 25:1*
Talents	*Mt 25:14*
Sheep and goats	*Mt 25:31*
Growth of seed	*Mk 4:26*
Household	*Mk 13:32*
Two debtors	*Lk 7:36*
Good Samaritan	*Lk 10:25*
Friend at midnight	*Lk 11:5*
Rich fool	*Lk 12:16*
Watchful servants	*Lk 12:35*
Faithful steward	*Lk 12:42*
Barren fig tree	*Lk 13:6*
Banquet	*Lk 14:15*
Counting the cost	*Lk 14:25*
Lost coin	*Lk 15:8*
Forgiving Father	*Lk 15:11*
Dishonest steward	*Lk 16:1*
Rich man and Lazarus	*Lk 16:19*
Master and servant	*Lk 17:7*
Widow	*Lk 18:1*
Pharisee and tax collector	*Lk 18:9*
Ten pounds	*Lk 19:11*
House built on rock	*Mt 7:24*
Leaven	*Mt 13:33*
Lost sheep	*Mt 18:12*
Lamp under a bushel	*Mk 4:21*
New cloth in old garment	*Mk 2:21*
New wine in old wineskins	*Mk 2:22*
Sower	*Mk 4:3*
Mustard seed	*Mk 4:30*
Vineyard	*Mk 12:1*
Leaves on fig tree	*Mk 13:28*

Day of Atonement
This is the most important Jewish festival. The High Priest used to offer sacrifices for the sins of the people *Lev 16:29–34*. It took place on the 10th day of Tishri (October).

Feast of Dedication
Its purpose was to celebrate the restoration and rededication of the temple by Judas Maccabeus in 165 B.C. *Jn 10:22*. It began on the 25th day of Chislev (December).

Feast of Passover
This celebrated the deliverance of the Hebrews from their captivity in Egypt, whereby the angel of death killed the first-born in Egyptian homes but 'passed over' the Hebrews' homes that had blood sprinkled on the door posts *Ex 12:23–27*. It took place on the 14th day of Nisan (April).

Day of Pentecost
This was the Jewish wheat harvest festival. The name *pentecost* was held 50 days after the Passover festival. It was held on the 6th of Sivan (May). *Acts 2:1*, *Jn 13:1*, *Lev 23:16*, *Deut. 16:10*.

Feast of Tabernacles
Also known as the Feast of Ingathering *Ex 23:16*. The purpose was to remember the time when the Hebrews lived in tents during the wilderness wanderings. It took place on the 15th of Tishri (October).

Business Hours

Shopping hours 8.30a.m. to 1 p.m. and 3p.m. to 7p.m. Moslem closed Friday, Jewish closed Saturday, and Christian closed Sunday.
VAT is 15%.

Banking hours: Sunday, Monday, Tuesday, Thursday, Friday 8.30a.m. to 12.30p.m.; Wednesday 4p.m. to 5.30p.m.; closed on Sunday.

Telephones

Tokens for the telephone can be purchased at post offices at 5 shekels each. Local calls 1 token. Inter-city one token every 20 seconds. Night rate 40 seconds. Dial 14 for information, 15 for wake-up service, (03) 625241 for weather report.

What to wear

On the tour, it is best for women to take a shawl or something similar, to cover the shoulders and arms, in order to gain admittance to holy places. It is considered inappropriate to have bare arms.

What to bring

A pocket Bible and notebook.

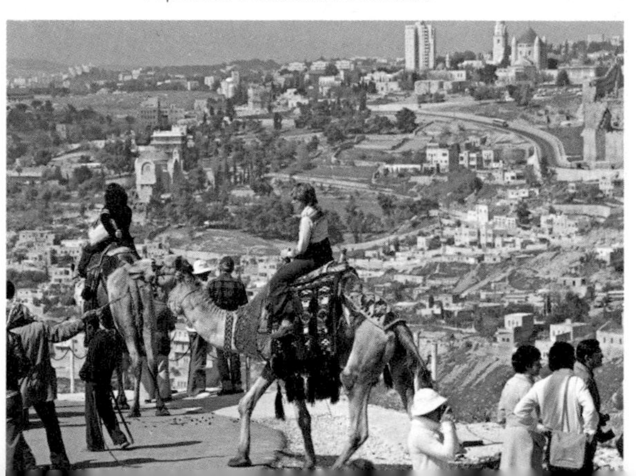

INDEX

Biblical names are printed in *italics* where they are different from the present-day names

BOOKS FOR FURTHER STUDY

Handbook to the Bible
Lion Publishing. A 680-page full-colour reference manual and commentary on the whole Bible. There are nearly 400 full-colour pictures, 68 maps and ready-reference lists. A must for study on your return from Israel.

Halley's Bible Handbook
Oliphants. A 500-page commentary, full of useful information about the Bible.

Fodor's Guide to Israel
Hodder & Stoughton. This general tourist guidebook is really the best book to purchase before going to Israel.

An Evangelical's Guidebook to the Holy Land Wayne DeHoney
Broadman Press.

Israel Guide Zev Vilnay
Available only in Israel for $15. This is the best introduction to Israel's sites from a Jewish point of view.

The Uniqueness of Israel Lance Lambert
Kingsway Publications. An inspiring survey of the history and geography of Israel.

Photographs in this book are reproduced by kind permission of the following:

Colour Library International — front cover.

Dr K. Linton — page 66.

Brunnen Verlag — pages 60, 82, 85, 88, all © Brunnen Publishing House, Giessen.

John Walden — pages 1, 15 *(top)*, 16, 17, 18, 19, 21, 22 *(top)*, 26 *(bottom)*, 29 *(top)*, 32, 35, 37-39, 41 *(top)*, 43-45, 48-55, 57-59, 64, 67, 68, 71, 72, 73, 75, 76, 83.

Holy Views Ltd (Jerusalem) — pages 11, 13, 15 *(bottom)*, 24 *(top)*, 25, 26 *(top)*, 29 *(bottom)*, 33, 34, 41 *(bottom)*, 47, 56, 78, 79, 80, 81.

T.L.D. Daisley — pages 8, 14, 20, 22 *(bottom)* © B.L. Services & Supplies, 24 *(bottom)*, 30 © B.L. Services & Supplies, 31 © Israel Colour Slides Co., 62, 65, 77.

Designed by Douglas Martin Associates

NOTES

NOTES

NOTES

NOTES

NAMES AND ADDRESSES OF TOUR COMPANIONS

NAMES AND ADDRESSES OF TOUR COMPANIONS